C000279680

EGGCORNS

For brave little Zoe

First published 2020 by The O'Brien Press Ltd,
12 Terenure Road East, Rathgar, Dublin 6, D06 HD27, Ireland
Tel: +353 1 4923333; Fax: +353 1 4922777
E-mail: books@obrien.ie
Website: www.obrien.ie
The O'Brien Press is a member of Publishing Ireland.

Published in

DUBLIN
UNESCO
City of Literature

ISBN: 978-1-78849-192-1

7 6 5 4 3 2 1
23 22 21 20

Printed and bound by Gutenberg Press, Malta.
The paper in this book is produced using pulp from managed forests.

EGGCORNS

FROM BUMBUM BEES TO JELLYCOPTERS

CHRIS JUDGE

THE O'BRIEN PRESS
DUBLIN

Foreword

I first heard the phrase 'eggcorns' in 2011, when it was a feature of the podcast by comedians Adam and Joe. They would read out hilarious mishearings and mispronunciations, made mostly by adults. In the following years, I became fascinated by mispronounced words and phrases uttered by my young nephews and nieces, and more recently by my own daughters, Joey and Juno. In July 2019, on a particularly wet and windy camping trip to Kerry in south-west Ireland, I decided to illustrate four of these and posted them on my social media accounts. I put the word out and asked if anyone else might have heard any eggcorns – originally named by linguistics professor Geoffrey Pullum in 2003 – their children may have said, so that I might illustrate them. I was overwhelmed when I received more than 1,000 replies. It was such a joy to get so many. Shortly thereafter, I was contacted by the wonderful team at The O'Brien Press about making these eggcorns into a book and, with the kind permission of all contributors, this is what you now hold in your hands. I hope you enjoy reading this as much as I did making it.

a lemon o'clock

blazer bean

blue barry

bumbum bee

button-up squash

buzz stop

carcodile

cat shoe nuts

caterpillow

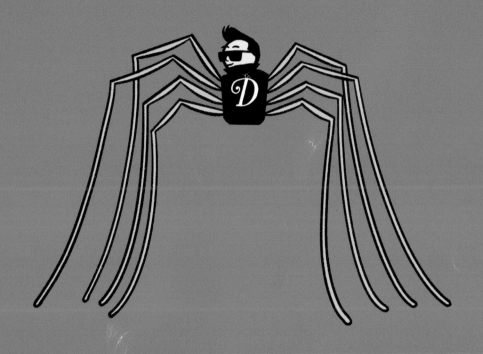

danny long legs

dinosaw

doggles

dolphant

earplane

egg phones

elelamp

funny wabbit

ginger bear man

high brows

hippobottomus

ice plop

jellycopter

kingcumber

long mower

meringuetan

mermalade

michaelwave

pianimal

prickled onion

pterodaffodil

puffalo

roller toaster

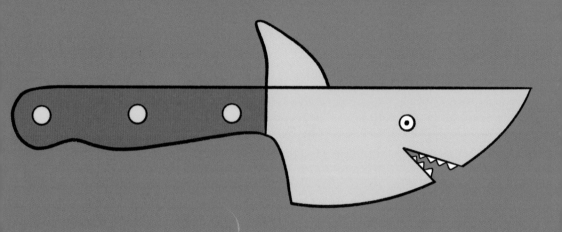

shark knife

sleeping brush

soup case

strawbaby

sun scream

tangle

waterlemon

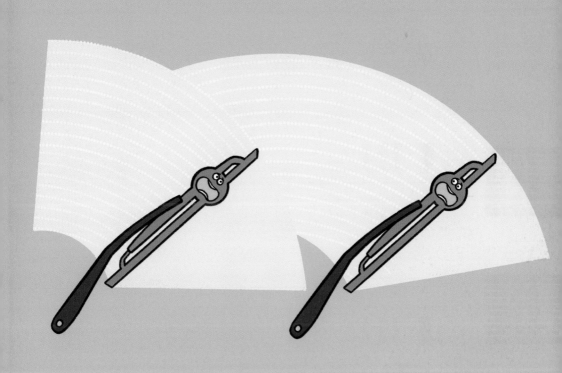

window wipe screamers

a lemon o'clock
(eleven o'clock)
Dash Jackson

blazer bean
(laser beam)
Casper

blue barry
(blueberry)
Juno

bumbum bee
(bumblebee)
Joey

button-up squash
(butternut squash)
Indigo Cooper

buzz stop
(bus stop)
Lindsey Bampton

carcodile
(crocodile)
Joey

cat shoe nuts
(cashew nuts)
Zayna Fakhani

caterpillow
(caterpillar)
Liz Little

danny long legs
(daddy-longlegs)
Annabelle Metcalfe

dinosaw
(dinosaur)
Lily Gorton

doggles
(goggles)
Joey

dolphant
(dolphin)
Naoise and Daire Barry

earplane
(aeroplane)
Fisher

egg phones
(headphones)
Juno

elelamp
(elephant)
Joey

funny wabbit
(bunny rabbit)
Odhrán Bonine

ginger bear man
(gingerbread man)
Juno

high brows
(eyebrows)
Juno

hippobottomus
(hippopotamus)
Rory Lyons

ice plop
(ice pop)
Joey

jellycopter
(helicopter)
Ivy

king cumber
(cucumber)
Clara Haigh

long mower
(lawn mower)
Ruairí Monaghan

meringuetan
(orang-utan)
Síofra McGarr

mermalade
(marmalade)
Ellie

michaelwave
(microwave)
Joshua Merrifield

pianimal
(animal)
John O'Herlihy

prickled onion
(pickled onion)
Clara Haigh

pterodaffodil
(pterodactyl)
Isabella Boyle

puffalo
(buffalo)
Stevie

roller toaster
(roller coaster)
Emilia Delgado

shark knife
(sharp knife)
Tom McBride

sleeping brush
(sweeping brush)
Juno

soup case
(suitcase)
Henry Fast

strawbaby
(strawberry)
Tadhg Bohill

sun scream
(sunscreen)
Maeve Mulvaney

tangle
(candle)
Joey

waterlemon
(watermelon)
Orlaith Lynn

window wipe screamers
(windscreen wipers)
Theo Bluer